# curiousabout
# BIGFOOT

T0005024

BY GILLIA M. OLSON

AMICUS • AMICUS INK

# What are you

## What Bigfoot Looks Like

PAGE
**4**

## How Bigfoot Acts

PAGE
**10**

# curious about?

CHAPTER **3** THREE

## Finding Bigfoot
PAGE
**14**

Curious About is published
by Amicus and Amicus Ink
P.O. Box 227
Mankato, MN 56002
www.amicuspublishing.us

Editor: Alissa Thielges
Designer: Kathleen Petelinsek
Photo researcher: Bridget Prehn

Library of Congress Cataloging-in-Publication Data
Names: Olson, Gillia M., author.
Title: Curious about bigfoot / Gillia M. Olson.
Description: Mankato : Amicus, [2022] | Series: Curious about
unexplained mysteries | Includes bibliographical references
and index. | Audience: Ages 6–9 | Audience: Grades 2–3
Identifiers: LCCN 2019053830 (print) | LCCN 2019053831
(ebook) | ISBN 9781681519807 (library binding) | ISBN
9781681526270 (paperback) | ISBN 9781645490654 (pdf)
Subjects: LCSH: Sasquatch—Juvenile literature.
Classification: LCC QL89.2.S2 O47 2022 (print) |
LCC QL89.2.S2 (ebook) | DDC 001.944—dc23
LC record available at https://lccn.loc.gov/2019053830
LC ebook record available at https://lccn.loc.gov/2019053831

Photos © Shutterstock/RikoBest cover; iStock/borchee
cover; Shutterstock/Daniel Eskridge 2, 6–7, 9;
Shutterstock/aleks1949 2, 10–11; Science Source/John
Sibbick 3, 16–17; Shutterstock/CineBlade 4–5; Shutterstock/
Michal Sanca 5; Shutterstock/Debbie Steinhausser 8; Kathleen
Petelinsek 12; Shutterstock/critterbiz 13; Shutterstock/
Paul Juser 14; Getty/Bettmann 15; Shutterstock/Nosyrevy
18 (man's foot); Shutterstock/Eliza Sandoval Cruzado
18 (Bigfoot's foot); Alamy/Gary Crabbe/Enlightened
Images 19; iStock/abadonian 20; iStock/GlobalP 21 (1);
Shutterstock/Ljupco Smokovski/21 (2), Jeffrey B. Banke 21
(3), D.O.F 21 (4), Shutterstock/wernermuellerschell 21 (5)

# CHAPTER ONE

# Is Bigfoot real?

**DID YOU KNOW?**
The Bigfoot Field Researchers Organization (BFRO) collects Bigfoot sightings. They have over 5,000 reports from the U.S.!

A mock sign warns that Bigfoot has been spotted in this area.

People have told Bigfoot **legends** for hundreds of years. Bigfoot goes by many names. The Coast Salish tribe has Sasquatch. In the mountains of Asia, there's the yeti. But legends aren't proof. No one has found scientific **evidence** of Bigfoot. It's good to keep asking questions.

# What does Bigfoot look like?

People in Asia have reported seeing a yeti in the mountains.

People say Bigfoot looks like a person mixed with an ape. It's very tall and walks on two legs. Most people say Bigfoot has black or brown fur. Bigfoots in different places might look different. The yeti is white. The yeren from China has red fur.

**DID YOU KNOW?**
Some reports say Bigfoot is twice as big as an average human.

12 ft (3.7 m)

6 ft (1.8 m)

Bigfoot          human

Skunk

# What does Bigfoot smell like?

A lot of people say Bigfoot stinks. It smells like a wild animal. In Florida, people see Bigfoots in the swamp. They stink really bad. People call these creatures skunk apes. They smell like skunk and dead fish, rolled up in garbage.

A painting shows
what a skunk ape
might look like.

# Does Bigfoot talk?

In most sightings, Bigfoot hides behind trees or shrubs.

Bigfoot seems to be quiet and shy. No one has caught one yet! Some reports say Bigfoot knocks on trees to send messages. It uses its fists or a stick. Another legend says Bigfoot has a call like a train whistle.

# What else could it be?

Lots of people see Bigfoot in areas where black bears also live. Black bears sometimes walk on their back legs. They can look like an ape person. Statues, large dogs, and hunters have all been mistaken for Bigfoot, too.

**DID YOU KNOW?**
Bigfoot sightings are often in the same area as black bears.

Black bear range
● Bigfoot sightings

A black bear standing on its back legs could look like Bigfoot.

# Where do people look for Bigfoot?

Willow Creek, California, is a tourist spot.

Some people go to the site of a famous short film. It was taken near Willow Creek, California, in 1967. The film shows a hairy creature walking. Was it Bigfoot? There's no proof. But about 7,000 people visit the area each year. People go "squatchin'," or Sasquatch hunting.

The Bigfoot in the 1967 film may have been someone in a costume.

# Has anyone found Bigfoot bones? Or hair?

Early humans watch a group of Gigantopithecus apes.

People thought they did. Most of the hair and bones were from other animals. The rest was too damaged to test.

People have found bones of Gigantopithecus. This giant ape lived 300,000 years ago. It was as big as a polar bear. Some Bigfoot hunters think this ape never died out.

# Has anyone faked seeing Bigfoot?

Yes, many people have. In 1958, loggers in California found big footprints. They called the creature that made them "Bigfoot." Ray Wallace, one of the loggers, made the tracks. No one knew until Wallace died in 2002. His children then said it had been a prank.

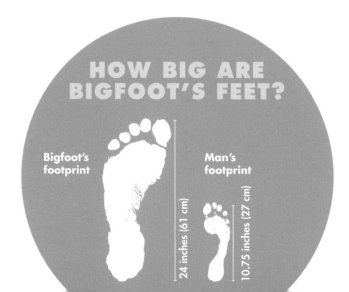

**HOW BIG ARE BIGFOOT'S FEET?**

Bigfoot's footprint

Man's footprint

24 inches (61 cm)

10.75 inches (27 cm)

This cast of a huge footprint is on display at a museum in Willow Creek, California.

Bob Titmus and Syl McCoy at Hyampom with casts of 17 inches, 16 inches and 15 inches in length.

in that part of the country, Bigfoot was back. Apparently the sight of logs flying up or down the hill with one end in the air really roused his curiosity, because for a while the tracks were around the machines every night.

Under the circumstances, Dave Blake, the logging operator, told me, it got difficult to keep men on the job. One evening the foreman wrote a note and stuck it on a log. When Blake asked him what he was doing he said, "I'm leaving a note for Bigfoot to come to work in the morning."

Besides the size of his feet, Bigfoot earned fame in 1958 for the feats of sheer strength he was reputed to have performed, which included throwing huge wheels from earthmovers and large-diameter culverts off the road into the creek, and tossing full drums of deisel fuel around.

I was never able to check very closely on any such stories at that time, but in 1967 I talked to four men, in three different towns, who had been working at the high-lead operation in 1963. They had all been greatly impressed by one particular incident that took place in mid morning not far from where crews were working.

26

As I un... all details ahead an... stalling... culvert... two cr... heard... vert... went... trai... cul... me... ho... t...

19

# Why do people believe in Bigfoot?

**If giant squids are real, could Bigfoot be?**

Other animal legends turn out to be real. **Kraken** legends probably came from giant squid. People had seen dead squid. But no one got a picture of a live one until 2005. What else might be out there?

**BROWN OR BLACK BEARS**

**1**

**PEOPLE IN FURRY COSTUMES**

**2**

**PEOPLE IN GHILLIE SUITS**

**3**

**ESCAPED CHIMPANZEES OR GORILLAS**

**4**

**MOOSE, ELK OR CARIBOU FROM BEHIND**

**5**

## ASK MORE QUESTIONS

**How many people believe Bigfoot is real?**

**Is there a way to prove Bigfoot exists?**

**Try a BIG QUESTION: Why do people believe in Bigfoot without solid evidence?**

## SEARCH FOR ANSWERS

**Search the library catalog or the Internet.**
A librarian, teacher, or parent can help you.

**Using Keywords**
Find the looking glass.

**Keywords are the most important words in your question.**

**If you want to know about:**
- belief in Bigfoot, type: BIGFOOT SURVEY
- proving Bigfoot exists, type: BIGFOOT PROOF

## FIND GOOD SOURCES

### Here are some good, safe sources you can use in your research.
Your librarian can help you find more.

### Books
**Bigfoot** by Bradley Cole, 2019.

**Bigfoot** by Jen Besel, 2020.

### Internet Sites
**Chapman University Survey: Paranormal America**
blogs.chapman.edu/wilkinson/2018/10 /16/paranormal-america-2018/
Universities (.edu sites) are good sources of research.

**PBS: It's Okay to Be Smart: Could Bigfoot Really Exist?**
www.pbs.org/video/its-okay-be-smart-bigfoot/
PBS is public television. Public television has great learning videos.

Every effort has been made to ensure that these websites are appropriate for children. However, because of the nature of the Internet, it is impossible to guarantee that these sites will remain active indefinitely or that their contents will not be altered.

## SHARE AND TAKE ACTION

### Protect nature for whatever animals might be out there.
Don't litter. Use less so you make less garbage.

### Visit a museum.
See fossils and learn about animals that have gone extinct.

### Ask a parent to take you camping in the woods.
Maybe go on your own Bigfoot hunt!

# GLOSSARY

**evidence** Things shown to prove a claim.

**ghillie suit** A type of camouflage clothing that is designed to look like the surrounding area to help a person blend in. Often used by the military, police, and hunters.

**Kraken** A legendary sea monster.

**legend** A story from the past whose truth is often accepted but cannot be checked.

**report** A spoken or written account of something that has been observed or investigated.

**sighting** The event of seeing something, especially something rare or hidden.

# INDEX

## About the Author

Gillia M. Olson is a skeptic by nature but loves all things paranormal nonetheless. She stays curious and open-minded and hopes you will, too. She lives in southern Minnesota with her husband and daughter.